The MONEY Flow Process

ISBN: 978-1-923476-55-4 (paperback)

Published in Australia by Jayne Victoria Moroni and InHouse Publishing.
www.inhousepublishing.com.au

A catalogue record for this book is available from the National Library of Australia

For my family — your love has been the steady heartbeat behind every dream I've dared to chase.

To those who believed in me long before I believed in myself — this is for you.

To my clients, past and present — your courage to transform inspired every word within these pages.

For the people walking the path of financial freedom — may this guide bring clarity, confidence, and calm.

For you, the reader — may this be the beginning of a new, empowered chapter in your life.

OUTLINE OF YOUR BOOK

INTRODUCTION: THE POWER OF SIMPLICITY IN MONEY MANAGEMENT

- Why financial stress is common but unnecessary
- How small, intentional changes create financial freedom
- The connection between money and mindset
- Overview of what readers will gain from this book

CHAPTER 1: THE MAGIC OF A SIMPLE BUDGET AND ACCOUNT AUTOMATION

- Why budgeting doesn't mean restriction — it means freedom
- How automation removes willpower struggles and decision fatigue
- Step-by-step guide to setting up automated systems for bills, savings, and spending
- Real-life example of a stress-free financial system in action

CHAPTER 2: PAYING OFF YOUR HOME LOAN SOONER AND SAVING THOUSANDS

- The cost of a standard 30-year mortgage vs paying it off early
- Strategies to shave years off your mortgage
- Making fortnightly instead of monthly payments
- Rounding up repayments
- Using an offset account or redraw facility
- Leveraging lump sum payments wisely
- Example scenarios showing how small changes can lead to big savings

CHAPTER 3: ALIGNING SPENDING WITH YOUR VALUES

- Why people feel guilty about spending money — and how to change that
- Identifying your core values and how they relate to money
- The "Value-Based Spending Plan" (spend where it matters, cut where it doesn't)
- Exercises to help readers define their personal money values

CHAPTER 4: THE POWER OF GOAL SETTING IN FINANCIAL SUCCESS

- How setting clear financial goals rewires your subconscious
- The link between vision, confidence, and

financial habits
- SMART financial goals vs vague dreams
- A goal-setting exercise to create clarity and motivation

CHAPTER 5: HOW COUPLES CAN ALIGN THEIR FINANCIAL GOALS AND STRENGTHEN THEIR RELATIONSHIP

- Why money is one of the biggest sources of relationship conflict
- The difference between financial values, habits, and beliefs
- How to have meaningful (and conflict-free) money conversations
- The "Financial Harmony Plan" is a step-by-step guide for couples to create shared goals and manage money together

CHAPTER 6: SHARPEN THE SAW (REVIEW, ADJUST, AND KEEP YOUR MONEY FLOWING)

- **Why Financial Success Isn't "Set and Forget"** – Why regular check-ins keep your money on track
- **Step 1: The 15-Minute Monthly Check-In** – Quick wins to review spending, bills, savings, mortgage, and celebrate progress
- **Step 2: The 6-Month Money Tune-Up** – A deeper review of income, expenses, savings goals, loans, and investments

- **Step 3: The Annual Financial Review** – Big-picture planning for goals, tax, super, and insurance
- **Step 4: Stay Flexible and Adjust** – Life isn't linear, so learn to reset and keep moving forward
- **Real-Life Example: Emma's Transformation** – How simple check-ins turned her finances around
- **Key Takeaways** – Consistency and small tweaks create long-term financial success

THE FINAL CHAPTER: YOUR MONEY MASTERY PLAN (TAKING ACTION AND LIVING FINANCIALLY FREE)

Why knowing isn't enough — it's the doing that creates transformation

- How to set up your automated "Money Flow System" so your finances run in the background
- Choosing your top three financial goals to create focus and momentum
- Aligning your spending with your values so money supports what truly matters to you
- Attacking debt with a proven strategy and building wealth with the right guidance
- The importance of regular money check-ins and simple adjustments to stay on track

- Why enjoying the journey is just as important as the destination
- Final thoughts, encouragement, and next steps for living financially free

CONCLUSION: FINANCIAL PEACE, SUCCESS, AND FREEDOM

- The mindset shift from scarcity to abundance
- How to maintain your financial systems for life
- Final words of encouragement and next steps

Introduction

THE POWER OF SIMPLICITY IN MONEY MANAGEMENT

Let's be real, money can feel like a necessary evil. You work hard for it, you try to save it, and yet somehow it always seems to vanish like socks in the laundry. But here's the good news: managing money doesn't have to be a complicated, stress-inducing chore. In fact, when you strip it down to the basics, financial success is surprisingly simple.

The problem? We've been taught that money is something to fear, stress over, or constantly chase. We see headlines about skyrocketing housing prices, hear horror stories about people drowning in debt, and get sucked into the comparison trap on social media. No wonder so many people feel financially stuck. But what if I told you that the secret to financial security isn't working harder or pinching every penny — it's creating a simple system that works for you?

That's exactly what this book is about. I'm here to show you how to:

- Build a budget so easy that it practically runs itself
- Automate your finances so you can stop

worrying about where your money is going
- Pay off your mortgage faster (and save a ridiculous amount of money in interest)
- Align your spending with your values so you never feel guilty about treating yourself
- Set goals that actually stick (no more wishful thinking)
- Work with your partner instead of against them when it comes to money

This is NOT another dry finance book telling you to cut out all the fun stuff and live like a monk. I fully support enjoying a good wine, taking vacations, and buying the fancy cheese. The goal here isn't to restrict yourself — it's to **take control** so you can spend guilt-free on the things that truly matter to you.

So, whether you're here because you want to stop living pay cheque to pay cheque, finally get ahead on your mortgage, or just feel like a financially responsible adult (without the constant stress), you're in the right place.

Let's dive in and make money simple, fun, and stress-free — yes, it's actually possible!

Chapter 1

THE MAGIC OF A SIMPLE BUDGET AND ACCOUNT AUTOMATION

WHY BUDGETING DOESN'T MEAN RESTRICTION — IT MEANS FREEDOM

Ah, budgeting. The word alone makes most people cringe, picturing spreadsheets, strict rules, and giving up their morning coffee like it's some kind of financial sacrificial ritual. But here's the thing — budgeting isn't about punishment. It's about **freedom**.

Think about it: When you don't know where your money is going, you constantly feel like you're running on a hamster wheel — earning, spending, wondering where it all went, repeat. But when you have a simple system in place, you get to **spend without guilt**, save without stress, and actually enjoy your money instead of feeling like it's slipping through your fingers.

A budget isn't a cage — it's a **game plan** that lets you control your money instead of your money controlling you. And the best part? You don't need to track every single cent or give up everything fun in life. You just need a system that works **on autopilot.**

Enter: Account Automation — Your Secret Weapon

Here's the reality: most people don't struggle with money because they don't earn enough. They struggle because their money isn't **organised**. It's like trying to run a kitchen where the milk is in the bathroom, the plates are in the garage, and the oven only works on Thursdays. Chaos.

The secret to making budgeting effortless is **automation**. Instead of manually paying bills, remembering savings transfers, or constantly questioning whether you can afford to go out for dinner, set up a system that does the thinking for you.

STEP-BY-STEP GUIDE TO AN AUTOMATED FINANCIAL SYSTEM

1. SET UP SEPARATE ACCOUNTS
    - **Bills Account**: Covers rent/mortgage, utilities, insurance, subscriptions, phone and internet, car/personal loan repayments, council rates, etc.
    - **Expenses Account:** Groceries and petrol
    - **Savings/Investing Account**: Because Future You deserves to be rich and happy.

- **Entertainment Account**: Going out, fast food, movies, pubs, dinners, etc.

***Note:* The Account your pay goes into**. I usually recommend this becomes your Expenses Account as it already has a card attached. However, if you have direct debits coming out of this account you can always make this your Bills Account. Make sure to check with your bank when working with offset accounts as you may be limited to only having a card on some of your offset accounts so you would want to make those accounts Expenses and Entertainment as you will need cards for those.

2. AUTOMATE YOUR BILLS AND SAVINGS FIRST

- Direct a set amount into your **Bills Account** each payday. This covers all fixed expenses.
- Direct a set amount into your **Expenses Account** to cover groceries and petrol.
- Direct a set amount into your **Entertainment Account**. Having a nominated amount for entertainment is a real eye opener for most people, as what they think they should be spending and what they are spending is usually miles apart. This is a great way to stop wasting money on things that don't matter.
- Then anything left in your budget should be set to go to your **Savings Account** — even if it's just a small amount to start.

3. MAXIMISE INTEREST SAVINGS WITH MULTIPLE OFFSET ACCOUNTS

- Instead of keeping your savings in regular bank accounts earning next to nothing, **use multiple offset accounts** linked to your mortgage.

Example:

- ***Offset 1: Bills Account:*** Money sits here until bills are due, and any direct debits can come out of this account, ideally monthly.
- ***Offset 2: Expenses Account:*** Groceries and petrol — this can be your transaction account, keep your money working for you on the days you don't spend.
- ***Offset 3: Savings Account:*** Cash reserves sitting in an offset still save you interest every day.
- ***Offset 4: Entertainment Account:*** Again, it keeps every dollar working against your home loan interest until you use it.

Note: The more money sitting in offset accounts, the less interest you pay, meaning you can shave years off your home loan without changing your lifestyle.

4. LET THE SYSTEM RUN AND ENJOY YOUR LIFE

- No more micromanaging money. No more "Oh crap, I forgot that bill was due!" moments. When a bill comes in, pay it straight away from the bills account. Just a simple, stress-free way to manage money **without thinking about it.**

A REAL-LIFE EXAMPLE OF A STRESS-FREE FINANCIAL SYSTEM WITH MULTIPLE OFFSET ACCOUNTS

Meet Lisa. Lisa used to wing it with her money. She'd get paid, spend freely, and then panic when bills were due. After setting up automation, here's how her payday looks now:

- Her salary lands in her **Expenses Offset Account.**
- Automatically, money transfers:
    - $1,500 into her **Bills Offset Account** (rent, phone, utilities, etc.).
    - $300 into **Savings Offset Account**, keeping her cash reserve but also reducing mortgage interest.
    - $500 into her **Entertainment Offset Account**.

- The rest stays in her **Expenses Offset Account** to cover groceries and petrol.

Now, Lisa never stresses about money, has savings growing automatically, and has even reduced her mortgage by five years just by using multiple offset accounts wisely. And guess what? She still buys her morning coffee.

KEY TAKEAWAYS

✓ A budget isn't about restriction — it's about financial freedom.

✓ Automating your money removes stress and decision fatigue.

✓ Using separate accounts keeps everything organised and effortless.

✓ Multiple offset accounts can slash years off your mortgage without extra effort.

✓ A simple system makes money easy — so you can focus on living life.

Chapter 2

PAYING OFF YOUR HOME LOAN SOONER AND SAVING THOUSANDS

THE 30-YEAR MORTGAGE TRAP (AND HOW TO ESCAPE IT)

Picture this: You take out a 30-year mortgage, pay your repayments like a responsible adult, and by the time you finally own your home outright, your kids have moved out, your dog has retired from fetching sticks, and you've handed over **hundreds of thousands of dollars in interest** to the bank. Sound fun? Didn't think so.

The truth is, most people **pay way more** than they need to for their homes. On average, you would have paid for two houses but only have one. I find it interesting from a psychological perspective that we are so trained to just accept paying double to a bank for the privilege of having our own home, but if you paid for two meals and only got one, you would say, "Hey, where's my other meal? I'm not accepting that." We have just accepted the bank's profit as the norm, but we shouldn't. I would much rather my clients have two houses than the banks have additional profits, simply because they don't realise how easy it is to cut down that loan term — and the total interest you pay the bank — by making a few smart moves. It's not hard, people!

Here's the kicker: **You don't need to be earning more money to do this. You just need to be strategic.**

HOW MUCH INTEREST ARE YOU ACTUALLY PAYING?

Let's break it down with a real example.

> Say you borrow **$600,000** at an interest rate of **6%** on a standard 30-year home loan.

- Monthly repayment: **$3,597**
- Total interest paid over 30 years: **$695,089** (ouch!)
- Total amount paid to the bank: **$1,295,089**

That means you're paying more in interest than the original loan amount. You essentially bought **TWO houses** — one for yourself and one for the bank. But what if you could cut **five, 10, or even 15 years off** your loan and save a **massive** chunk of that interest?

Good news — you can. And it's easier than you think.

SIMPLE STRATEGIES TO PAY OFF YOUR MORTGAGE FASTER

1. SWITCH TO FORTNIGHTLY REPAYMENTS

This is the **easiest hack** that can save you **years** off your loan. Instead of making **monthly** repayments, switch to **fortnightly**.

- There are 12 months in a year, but **26 fortnights**.
- That means you'll be making **one extra monthly** repayment per year without even noticing.
- For our example, this could cut **more than four years** off your loan and save you over **$90,000 in interest**.

Effort required: None. Just switch your repayment schedule.

2. ROUND UP YOUR REPAYMENTS

If your repayment is $3,597, round it up to **$3,700** or **$3,800**.

- Just an extra **$100 per month** could **take three years** off your loan.
- If you can stretch it to **$200 per month**, you'll save over **$75,000 in interest**.

Small change, *huge impact*.

3. USE AN OFFSET ACCOUNT (OR MULTIPLE OFFSETS!)

Instead of letting your savings sit in an account

earning 1–2% interest, put them in an offset account linked to your mortgage. Every dollar sitting there reduces the interest you pay.

Example:

> If you have **$50,000** sitting in your offset account, that's **$50,000 less** you're paying interest on.
>
> - Over 30 years, this alone could save you **$150,000+ in interest** and shave **five to seven years** off your loan.
> - Multiple offset accounts = even **greater** flexibility and savings.

4. THROW WINDFALLS AT YOUR MORTGAGE

Got a **tax refund**? A **bonus** at work? An **inheritance** from Great-Aunt Susan? Instead of blowing it all on a last-minute trip to Bali, throw a chunk at your home loan.

- A **$10,000 lump sum** paid early in your loan can save you **tens of thousands** in interest.
- Even small one-off payments make a difference over time.

5. REFINANCE TO A LOWER RATE (AND KEEP YOUR REPAYMENTS THE SAME)

Interest rates change. Banks compete. That means you should *NEVER* stay on the same home loan for 30 years.

- A **0.5% lower rate** can save you **tens of thousands** over your loan's life.
- Refinancing every few years ensures you always have a competitive rate. Although remember that when you refinance you need to ensure you are keeping to your existing loan term and not increasing it back out to 30 years or you will be going backwards.

PRO TIP:
When you refinance to a lower rate, keep making the same higher repayments as before. You'll pay your loan off much faster without even feeling it.

A REAL-LIFE EXAMPLE OF THESE STRATEGIES IN ACTION

Meet Dave and Sarah. They took out a **$600,000** mortgage at 6%.

BEFORE:

- Monthly repayments: **$3,597**
- Loan term: **30 years**
- Total interest paid: **$695,089**

AFTER:

✓ Switched to **fortnightly repayments.** Cut four years off the loan.

✓ Rounded up their **repayments by $200/ month.**

Cut three more years off.
✓ Put **$40,000 in an offset** account. Cut six more years off.
✓ Refinanced to a **lower interest rate** after five years. Cut another five years off.

TOTAL YEARS SAVED: 18
TOTAL INTEREST SAVED: OVER $300,000

Now they'll own their home in **12 years instead of 30**, and they've saved enough to take that **trip to Bali every year** if they want to.

KEY TAKEAWAYS

✓ A 30-year mortgage is **optional** — you can pay it off much sooner.

✓ Small changes (like fortnightly payments and rounding up) make **a massive difference.**

✓ Offset accounts are your **best friend** for slashing interest costs.

✓ Refinancing keeps you ahead and can **save you thousands.**

Your mortgage doesn't have to last forever — unless you want to gift your bank a holiday home on your behalf.

Chapter 3

ALIGNING SPENDING WITH YOUR VALUES (SO YOU NEVER FEEL LIKE YOU'RE WASTING MONEY)

WHY DO WE FEEL GUILTY ABOUT SPENDING?

Ever bought something and then felt **instant regret**? Maybe it was a $300 air fryer you swore would change your life (but now just collects dust), or that fancy gym membership you barely use because deep down, you'd rather take long walks with a coffee in hand.

On the flip side, have you ever spent a **ridiculous amount of money on something**, but felt **zero guilt** because it truly made you happy? Maybe it was an overseas trip, a beautiful piece of art, or a first-class ticket just to experience the good life.

The difference? When spending aligns with your **values**, it feels amazing. When it doesn't, it feels like a waste.

The problem is, most of us spend on autopilot, without **consciously** deciding what actually matters to us. And that's where our money starts to feel like it's disappearing into a black hole.

So, let's change that.

STEP 1: IDENTIFY YOUR CORE MONEY VALUES

Your financial values are **personal** — they're about what truly brings you joy, fulfilment, and a sense of purpose.

Grab a piece of paper and answer this:

> What are the **top three things** that bring you happiness in life?
>
> It could be freedom, security, adventure, family, creativity, health, personal growth, generosity — whatever matters most to you.

Now, let's align your spending with those values.

STEP 2: MATCH YOUR SPENDING TO YOUR VALUES

Here's how this works in real life:

> If you value freedom, mindless shopping sprees and piling on debt might actually stress you out. But spending on experiences,

travel, and investments that give you more life choices? That's money well spent.

If you value family, splurging on dinners out every night may feel wasteful, but investing in quality time with your loved ones (like a family holiday or setting up a cozy home) will feel incredibly fulfilling.

If you value health, spending on cheap fast food might feel like throwing money away, but prioritising a gym membership, organic groceries, or a wellness retreat might feel totally worth it.

The key is to consciously redirect spending from things that don't align with your values to the things that do.

STEP 3: THE "JOY VS OBLIGATION" TEST

Next time you're about to buy something, ask yourself:

Does this purchase bring me genuine joy, or am I doing it out of habit/pressure?

- If the answer is joy, go for it (guilt-free!).
- If it's an obligation — pause, rethink, and redirect those dollars towards what truly matters to you.

STEP 4: CUT THE STUFF THAT DOESN'T SERVE YOU (WITHOUT FEELING DEPRIVED)

Most people fail at budgeting because they focus on **cutting everything,** instead of just cutting what doesn't matter.

Take a look at your past three months of spending and ask:

✏ What did I spend money on that **didn't actually make me happy**?

Maybe it's:

- ✖ Subscriptions you never use.
- ✖ Daily takeaway coffee when you actually enjoy making it at home.
- ✖ Impulse shopping that sits in your wardrobe unworn.
- ✖ Fancy dinners out when you'd rather have a cozy night in.

Now redirect that money into what you actually love.

Imagine: Instead of feeling restricted, your budget now **empowers you** to spend on things that bring you happiness, while cutting out what doesn't.

This is how you stop feeling like money is "wasted" and start feeling like every dollar is working for your dream life.

A REAL-LIFE EXAMPLE: SARAH'S SPENDING MAKEOVER

BEFORE:
Sarah felt like she was constantly broke, even though she earned decent money. After reviewing her spending, she realised:

- She was spending $450/month on random online shopping that didn't make her happy.
- She had four different streaming subscriptions, but only used one.
- She was eating out more than five times a week, even though she actually enjoyed cooking.

AFTER:
She cut $600 of wasteful spending and redirected it towards:

✓ A monthly weekend getaway (something she always wished she could afford). $200.

✓ Saving or investing an extra $300/month into her future.

✓ Saving up for a dream trip to Italy (instead of spending money on things she didn't care about). $100.

Suddenly, Sarah felt wealthier — not because she earned more, but because every dollar now worked toward things that actually brought her joy.

KEY TAKEAWAYS

- ✓ Spending guilt disappears when your money aligns with your values.
- ✓ The "Joy vs Obligation" test helps you make better spending decisions.
- ✓ Cut what doesn't serve you — without sacrificing what makes you happy.
- ✓ Redirecting money into what **truly matters** makes you feel financially empowered.

Chapter 4

THE POWER OF GOAL SETTING IN FINANCIAL SUCCESS

WHY MOST FINANCIAL GOALS FAIL (AND HOW TO FIX THAT)

Ever set a New Year's resolution like ***"I'm going to save more money this year"*** or ***"I want to be better with my finances"***, only to completely forget about it by February?

Yeah, you're not alone.

The problem isn't you — it's the **way** you set the goal.

Most financial goals fail because they're **vague, uninspiring, or feel too far away** to matter. But when you learn how to set goals in a way that actually **programmes your subconscious mind for success,** everything changes.

Let's break it down.

THE SCIENCE BEHIND GOAL SETTING (AND HOW YOUR BRAIN PLAYS ALONG)

Your brain is basically a high-powered GPS system.

- When you give it clear, specific directions (a strong goal), it works overtime to find ways to make it happen.
- But if you give it a vague, wishy-washy goal ("I want to be better with money"), it gets confused and does nothing.

Think about it: If you enter "somewhere nice" into Google Maps, you're going **nowhere**. But if you enter "The Ritz in Paris" as your destination? Boom — directions, ETA, and even the best route appear.

Your brain works **exactly the same way**. So, let's get specific.

STEP 1: CREATE SMART FINANCIAL GOALS

The best goals follow the SMART formula:

- ✓ **Specific**: What exactly do you want to achieve?
- ✓ **Measurable**: How will you track progress?
- ✓ **Achievable**: Is it realistic for you?
- ✓ **Relevant**: Does it align with your values and life goals?
- ✓ **Time-bound**: When will you achieve it?

Example of a weak goal vs a strong goal:

- ✕ **Weak:** I want to save more money.
- ✓ **Strong:** I will save $10,000 by 31 December by putting $500/month into my high-interest savings account.

The second goal is crystal clear, has a deadline, and tells your brain exactly what needs to happen.

Now it has a destination — and your subconscious will start working to make it happen.

STEP 2: PROGRAM YOUR BRAIN WITH VISUAL CUES

Your subconscious mind is driven by **images and emotions**. That's why vision boards, affirmations, and writing down your goals actually work.

Here's how to supercharge your financial goals:

- ✓ **Write them down**: Physically writing your goal tells your brain, "This goal is important."
- ✓ **Use visuals**: Create a vision board with images of what achieving your goal looks like (dream home, travel, debt-free living).
- ✓ **Feel the success**: Close your eyes and imagine how you'll feel **once you've achieved it**.

Your brain will start **looking for ways** to make your goal a reality — sometimes without you even realising it.

STEP 3: BREAK IT DOWN INTO BITE-SIZED ACTIONS

Big financial goals can feel **overwhelming**, which is why most people give up before they even start.

Solution? Break them into tiny, easy steps.

Example: Paying off $20,000 in debt

- ***Step 1:*** Write down all debts and their interest rates.
- ***Step 2:*** Choose a strategy (Snowball, smallest debt vs Avalanche method, highest interest first).
- ***Step 3:*** Automate an extra $100/ month toward the highest-priority debt.
- ***Step 4:*** Track progress every month and celebrate small wins.
- ***Step 5:*** Once one debt is gone, roll that payment into the next one.

Suddenly, the big, scary goal becomes a series of small, doable actions.

And small actions? They add up fast.

STEP 4: THE "WHY" FACTOR (YOUR SECRET WEAPON)

Here's the truth: Money goals only stick if they're emotionally meaningful to you.

It's not just about saving money — it's about why you want to save it.

- ✓ Do you want to be debt-free so you can quit the job you hate?
- ✓ Are you saving for a home so your family has security?
- ✓ Do you want financial freedom so you never have to stress about bills again?

The stronger your **WHY**, the more motivated you'll be to stick with it.

So, when setting a financial goal, ask yourself:

Why does this goal matter to me?

If the answer doesn't make you feel something, it's not strong enough. Keep digging until it does.

A REAL-LIFE EXAMPLE: JAMES' $50K TURNAROUND

James was in **$50,000 of credit card debt** and felt like he'd never get out. He tried setting a goal before, but nothing stuck.

Then he **did it differently**:

- He got **specific**: "I will pay off $50,000 in three years."
- He made it **emotional**: "So I can stop stressing and take my kids on holiday every year."
- He created a **plan**: Cut expenses, side hustle, and automate extra repayments.
- He put **visual reminders** everywhere — a picture of the beach he'd take his kids to once he was debt-free.

Result? He smashed his goal in **2.5 years**, saved ***thousands in interest***, and now lives debt-free.

Because when you connect money with a **powerful "why"**, everything changes.

KEY TAKEAWAYS

✓ Most financial goals fail because they're too vague.

✓ Your brain is a GPS — it needs clear directions to work.

✓ SMART goals make your financial dreams tangible and achievable.

✓ Visualising success and making it emotional increases motivation.

✓ Small, consistent actions lead to massive results over time.

Chapter 5

HOW COUPLES CAN ALIGN THEIR FINANCIAL GOALS AND STRENGTHEN THEIR RELATIONSHIP

WHY MONEY IS ONE OF THE BIGGEST RELATIONSHIP STRESSORS

If love is blind, money is the flashing neon sign that says, *"Hey, we need to talk!"*

Money is one of the **top reasons why couples fight**, and it's not because one person is "bad with money" and the other is a financial guru. It's because **money is emotional**.

Think about it:

- ✓ Money represents **security** for some and **freedom** for others.
- ✓ Some people are **savers**, others are **spenders**.
- ✓ Some grew up in homes where money

was **scarce**, while others were taught **abundance**.

So, when you put two people together with different money habits, values, and emotions — you've got the **perfect storm for financial tension**.

But guess what? It doesn't have to be this way.

In fact, when couples get on the same financial page, money becomes a tool for **connection, teamwork, and building** an incredible future **together**. Let's talk about how to do it.

STEP 1: UNDERSTAND EACH OTHER'S MONEY MINDSET

Before you even talk **numbers**, you need to talk **history**. Ask each other these questions:

- What was money like in your house growing up? (Was it stressful? Comfortable?)
- Do you see money as something to **save** or something to **enjoy**?
- What's your biggest **financial fear**?
- What's your ultimate **money dream**?

These conversations **will change everything**.

Instead of judging your partner's money habits, you'll start to understand **why** they think and act the way they do.

And when you understand someone's **money story**, it's way easier to create a financial plan that works for **both** of you.

STEP 2: SET SHARED GOALS (INSTEAD OF FIGHTING OVER SPENDING)

Most financial arguments happen because one person says, "We should save more!" and the other says, "We should enjoy life more!"

Here's the secret: **You don't have to pick one**.

The goal is to create a financial plan that supports **BOTH** of your values.

- **The saver** wants security.
- **The spender** wants enjoyment.
- **The compromise?** A plan that builds wealth while still allowing guilt-free spending on the things that matter.

HOW TO SET SHARED FINANCIAL GOALS AS A COUPLE:

- *Step 1*: **Individually, write down your top three financial priorities**. Saving, travel, buying a house, investing, early retirement — whatever matters to you.
- *Step 2*: **Share your lists with each other**. Find common ground (or at least compromise).

- ***Step 3*: Create three joint financial goals** you're **BOTH** excited about.
- ***Step 4*: Set up separate accounts for each goal and automate contributions.**

Example:

- "We'll save for our first home while still setting aside money for a yearly holiday."
- "We'll invest $500/month for the future while keeping a 'Fun Money' account for guilt-free spending."

Why this works: When money is working toward both of your values, there's less stress and resentment — and more motivation to reach those goals together.

STEP 3: SET UP A SIMPLE AND CONFLICT-FREE MONEY SYSTEM

Want to avoid money fights? Take emotions out of the equation with a structured system. Here's a simple joint money system that works for most couples:

- ***Step 1*: Have a "Bills and Essentials" Account (Non-Negotiables)**

  ✓ Mortgage/rent

  ✓ Utilities

  ✓ Groceries

  ✓ Insurance

Each person contributes based on their income. If one partner earns more, they might cover a **higher percentage** of the bills instead of splitting 50/50.

- ***Step 2*: Have Separate "Fun Money" Accounts**

  ✓ Each person gets an individual spending account that they can use **without guilt or questioning**.

  ✓ No more ***"Why did you buy that?"*** arguments.

This **eliminates control issues**, allowing both partners financial freedom within a structured plan.

- ***Step 3*: Have Joint "Savings and Goals" Accounts**

Want to save for a home, travel, or retirement? Set up **joint savings accounts** for each goal and automate contributions.

Example:

✓ Home Deposit Fund

✓ Travel Fund

✓ Investing Fund

Now, instead of arguing about **whether** to save or spend, you're both actively working toward financial security **and** enjoying life.

- ***STEP 4*: Schedule A Monthly Money Date (Yes, With Wine!)**

Talking about money doesn't have to be awkward or stressful.

Instead, make it fun with a **monthly money date** where you:

✓ Pour a glass of wine (or coffee).

✓ Check in on your shared financial goals.

✓ Celebrate wins, adjust plans, and discuss upcoming expenses.

The goal? To stay financially aligned **without nagging, stress, or tension**.

A REAL-LIFE EXAMPLE: HOW JESS AND TOM STOPPED FIGHTING ABOUT MONEY

BEFORE:

- Jess (the saver) constantly stressed about money. Tom (the spender) felt controlled.
- Every month, they'd argue about **how much Tom spent on takeout** and **how much Jess wanted to save**.
- Tom felt judged. Jess felt unheard.

AFTER:

✓ They set up a **joint Bills Account** for all essentials.

✓ They created **separate "Fun Money" accounts**, so Tom could spend guilt-free while Jess saved without frustration.

✓ They automated **monthly savings toward a home and travel fund**.

✓ They started having **money dates** — and for the first time, **money became a positive topic instead of a fight**.

Now, instead of money being a point of tension, it's something they tackle together.

KEY TAKEAWAYS

✓ Money stress in relationships comes from different backgrounds, not bad habits.

✓ Understanding each other's **money mindset** leads to better communication.

✓ A joint financial plan should support **both partners' values**.

✓ Separate "Fun Money" accounts reduce money fights.

✓ A simple **joint money system** makes finances **easy and stress-free**.

✓ Monthly **money dates** keep you aligned and in control.

Chapter 6

SHARPEN THE SAW (REVIEW, ADJUST, AND KEEP YOUR MONEY FLOWING)

WHY FINANCIAL SUCCESS ISN'T "SET AND FORGET"

Here's a truth bomb: ***Even the best financial plan in the world will fail if you never check in on it.***

Think of your finances like a car. You wouldn't drive for years without servicing it, checking the oil, or making sure the wheels aren't about to fall off. Yet, most people do exactly that with their money. They set up a budget, automate their bills, and then **never look at it again**.

But life changes.

- You get a raise.
- Interest rates go up or down.
- You find new goals that excite you.
- Or, let's be honest — sometimes you just get a bit off track.

That's why **regular financial check-ins are crucial**.

They're not about "fixing" anything; they're about **optimising** what's already working and making sure your money is still moving in the right direction.

The good news? This doesn't have to be boring or time-consuming. A simple **15-minute check-in once a month** can keep your finances sharp and stress-free.

STEP 1: THE MONTHLY 15-MINUTE FINANCIAL CHECK-IN

Set aside 15 minutes once a month (ideally on your Money Date!) to go through these quick steps:

- ***Step 1*: Review Your Budget and Spending**
  - Look at your spending from the last month.
  - Did your money align with your values? (Or did Uber Eats win again?)
  - Adjust anything that feels out of whack.
- ***Step 2*: Check Your Bills and Subscriptions**
  - Are you still using everything you're paying for?
  - Is there a cheaper deal on utilities, phone plans, or insurance?
- ***Step 3*: Review Your Savings and Investments**
  - Are you on track with your savings goals?
  - Can you bump up your savings or investment contributions?

- *Step 4*: **Look at Your Mortgage and Interest Rates**
  - Could refinancing save you money?
  - Is your offset account working for you?

- *Step 5*: **Celebrate Your Wins!**
  - Did you hit a savings milestone?
  - Did you reduce debt?
  - Did you stick to your financial plan?
  - Treat yourself (guilt-free) for making progress!

Bonus Tip: Set a calendar reminder for your financial check-in. That way, you'll never forget!

STEP 2: THE 6-MONTH DEEP DIVE (MONEY TUNE-UP)

Every six months, take a **deeper dive** into your finances. This is like a **full car service** instead of just topping up the fuel.

WHAT TO REVIEW EVERY SIX MONTHS:

✓ **Your Income:** Has it increased? If so, where can you allocate extra money?

✓ **Your Expenses:** Are you overspending in areas that don't align with your values?

✓ **Your Savings Goals:** Are they still relevant, or do you need to adjust?

✓ **Your Mortgage and Loans:** Could refinancing or debt consolidation save you money?

✓ **Your Investments:** Are you growing your wealth or just saving?

This check-in keeps you **intentional** about your financial future and ensures you're always optimising for success.

STEP 3: THE ANNUAL FINANCIAL REVIEW (BIG PICTURE THINKING)

Once a year, go **big picture** with your money. This is where you:

✓ Set new **financial goals** for the year ahead.

✓ Look at **tax strategies** to maximise your savings.

✓ Review your **superannuation/retirement plan**.

✓ Check your **insurance coverage** (life, income, health) to make sure it still fits your needs.

Think of this as your **"Money New Year"** — a fresh start where you can upgrade your financial game.

STEP 4: STAY FLEXIBLE AND ADJUST AS NEEDED

Here's a reality check: ***Life isn't linear***.

Some months, you'll smash your financial goals. Other months, life will throw curveballs (unexpected expenses, job changes, surprise adventures).

And that's OK.

The goal isn't to be perfect — it's to be consistent.

If you ever feel off track, just reset and keep moving forward. Financial success isn't about never making mistakes; it's about course-correcting quickly and staying focused on what really matters.

A REAL-LIFE EXAMPLE: HOW EMMA USED CHECK-INS TO TRANSFORM HER FINANCES

Emma used to feel completely out of control with money. She was earning well, but had no idea where her money was going. Every time she tried to budget, she'd give up after a few weeks.

Then, she started doing monthly **15-minute check-ins**.

- ***Month 1:*** She realised she was spending **$400/ month on subscriptions** she barely used. She cancelled half of them.
- ***Month 3:*** She adjusted her savings strategy and bumped up her mortgage repayments.

- *Month 6:* She reviewed her home loan and **switched to a lower rate**, saving **$3,500 per year** in interest.
- *Year 1:* She hit her first **$10,000 savings goal** — something she never thought was possible.

Now, Emma feels **completely in control of her finances** — not because she micromanages every dollar, but because she **checks in regularly and makes small, powerful tweaks** along the way.

KEY TAKEAWAYS

✓ Financial success isn't **set and forget** — it's about regular check-ins.

✓ A **15-minute monthly review** keeps your money on track.

✓ A **6-month deep dive** helps you optimise your budget, mortgage, and investments.

✓ An **annual financial review** keeps you focused on big-picture wealth-building.

✓ **Flexibility is key** — life happens, and adjusting is part of the journey.

Final Chapter

YOUR MONEY MASTERY PLAN (TAKING ACTION AND LIVING FINANCIALLY FREE!)

THE DIFFERENCE BETWEEN KNOWING AND DOING

Let's be real — most people know they should budget, save, invest, and pay off debt faster. But knowing isn't the problem. **It's the doing that changes everything.**

You didn't pick up this book just to collect information — you picked it up because you want **real, lasting change**.

The good news? You don't have to do everything at once. The key to financial transformation is **small, consistent actions** that build momentum.

So, let's turn all this knowledge into a simple, **step-by-step Money Mastery Plan** that you can start using **right now**.

STEP 1: CREATE YOUR MONEY FLOW SYSTEM

Go back to **Chapter 1** and set up your **automated money flow**:

- ✓ **Multiple bank accounts** (Bills, Expenses, Savings, and Entertainment Offset Accounts).
- ✓ **Automate payments** for bills, savings, and investments.
- ✓ **Redirect spending** so money flows effortlessly toward your goals.

Why? Because when your money is working for you in the background, financial stress disappears.

STEP 2: CHOOSE YOUR TOP THREE FINANCIAL GOALS

In Chapter 4, we talked about setting clear, specific financial goals. Now, choose your top three.

Example:

- ✓ Pay off my credit card debt by December.
- ✓ Save $10,000 for my emergency fund in 12 months.
- ✓ Increase my mortgage repayments by $200 per month to save five years off my loan.

Why? Because when you focus on a few **powerful**

goals instead of trying to do everything, you're more likely to succeed.

STEP 3: ALIGN YOUR SPENDING WITH YOUR VALUES

Go back to Chapter 3 and make sure your money is flowing toward what actually matters to you.

Ask yourself:

- Does my spending make me happy, or am I wasting money on things I don't care about?
- What can I cut that doesn't serve me, and where can I redirect that money?

Why? Because when you align money with what brings you joy, you stop feeling guilty about spending.

STEP 4: ATTACK DEBT AND BUILD WEALTH

Depending on where you're at, decide:

If you have debt → Create a plan to pay it off faster.

If you're debt-free → Start investing and growing wealth.

- Debt Strategy: Choose Snowball (smallest first) or Avalanche (highest interest first) and automate extra repayments.

- Investing Strategy: Before jumping into investing, consult a financial planner. Their entire career is built around maximising wealth, and they can educate you on the best investment strategy tailored to your circumstances — whether that's shares, property, or other asset classes. Getting the right advice early on can save you years of trial and error and help you make informed, confident decisions about your financial future.

Why? Because wealth isn't just about how much you earn — it's about how well you use what you have.

STEP 5: CHECK IN REGULARLY AND ADJUST AS NEEDED

✓ Use the **15-minute monthly** check-in from **Chapter 6**:

✓ Look at your spending.

✓ Adjust where needed. Celebrate your wins.

And every **six months**, do a deeper financial tune-up to make sure you're still on track.

Why? Because financial success isn't about perfection — it's about **consistently staying engaged with your money**.

STEP 6: ENJOY THE JOURNEY!

Money is meant to give you **freedom, not stress**. The whole point of mastering your finances is so you can **live life on your terms**.

That means:

- ✓ Saying **yes** to opportunities that excite you.
- ✓ Feeling secure in your future.
- ✓ Knowing your money is working **for you**, instead of you working for money.

And most importantly — it means knowing that you are **in control**.

No more stress. No more uncertainty. Just a **simple, empowering money system** that supports your dream life.

FINAL THOUGHTS: YOU'VE GOT THIS!

If you take **just one** thing from this book, let it be this:

> ***Financial freedom isn't about how much you earn — it's about how well you use what you have.***

You don't need to be a millionaire to feel financially secure. You just need a plan, a system, and the **confidence to take control of your money**.

So, are you ready to live a life of **financial freedom, security, and success**?

IT STARTS TODAY.

Go set up your accounts, choose your goals, and take that first step.

The future **wealthy, stress-free, and empowered YOU** is waiting.

THE END... OR JUST THE BEGINNING?

This isn't really the end — it's the beginning of your financial transformation.

- ✓ If this book helped you, share it with someone you love.
- ✓ If you ever feel stuck, just come back to this book — your Money Mastery Plan is always here for you.

Now, go out there and **live your best (financially free) life**!

Next Steps

WANT MORE SUPPORT?

Power Mortgages isn't just about getting you a home loan or doing a fast refinance. I am passionate about helping my clients understand their goals and help them to achieve them. I specialise in helping people gain back control of their own finances. I do one on one sessions with clients to help them set a budget, create their "Money Flow" process and keep in touch with them to keep them motivated towards financial success. My goal is to make as many people understand that the system is designed to make them fail financially, only through understanding your values, setting goals and having a system will you break the cycle of debt and struggle and live the way we are all supposed to, confident, peaceful and free.

Reach out to me if you would like to start your journey to financial success

www.powermortgages.com.au

♡ Thank You

Thank you so much for taking the time to read this resource. Your support means the world to me and my small family business here in Western Australia.

I'm deeply passionate about helping people feel confident, in control, and excited about their money — and I'm so grateful to be a part of your journey.

If you'd like more resources, tools, or support, please don't hesitate to reach out:

📩 jayne@powermortgages.com.au

And if you found value in what you've read, I'd truly appreciate your feedback or a quick review. Let me know what resonated most or what you'd love to learn more about next!

With gratitude,

Jayne Victoria
Founder: Power Mortgages

About the Author

Jayne Victoria is a seasoned mortgage broker with over 14 years of experience in the finance industry. Throughout her career, she has assisted countless clients in achieving the dream of homeownership. However, she noticed a recurring pattern: many homeowners would "set and forget" their mortgages, ultimately paying nearly double the original loan amount over 30 years.

Driven by a passion to disrupt this cycle, Jayne founded **Power Mortgages**, a company dedicated to empowering individuals to take control of their financial futures. Combining her extensive knowledge in finance with certifications in Neuro-Linguistic Programming **(NLP)** and **Hypnosis**, she offers a holistic approach to wealth activation. Her mission is to help clients reduce the interest paid to banks, pay out their home loans sooner, and establish financial systems that lead to security and personalised wealth—whatever that means to them.

In *The Money Flow Process*, Jayne shares her insights and strategies to transform the way readers perceive and manage their finances. Her approach is not just about numbers; it's about redefining one's relationship with money to achieve true financial freedom.

Made in United States
Orlando, FL
04 November 2026

90201165R00036